Why Groups Go to Extremes

Why Groups Go to Extremes

Cass R. Sunstein

The AEI Press

Publisher for the American Enterprise Institute
WASHINGTON, D.C.

Library of Congress Cataloging-in-Publication Data

Sunstein, Cass R.
  Why groups go to extremes / Cass R. Sunstein.
      p. cm.
Includes bibliographical references.
    ISBN-13: 978-0-8447-4267-0 (pbk.)
    ISBN-10: 0-8447-4267-8
    1. Radicals—United States. 2. Radicalism—United States. I. Title.

    HN90.R3S85 2008
    303.48'4—dc22

                                                    2008024282

12 11 10 09 08   1 2 3 4 5

Contents

ACKNOWLEDGMENTS   vii

FOREWORD, *Robert Hahn*   ix

WHY GROUPS GO TO EXTREMES   1

The Basic Phenomenon *1*
Citizens *3*
Federal Judges and Polarized Differences *4*
Juries *7*
Why Polarization? Some Explanations *10*
  Information Strengthens Antecedent Beliefs 10
  Corroboration Breeds Confidence, Which Breeds Extremism 10
  Social Comparisons Shift Positions 11
Polarization and Democracy *12*
  Polarizing Events and Polarization Entrepreneurs 13
  Outgroups 13
  Feuds, Ethnic and International Strife, and War 14
  The Internet, Communications Policy, and Mass Deliberation 15
Deliberative Trouble *16*
Why Deliberate? *18*
The Virtues of Heterogeneity *19*
Enclave Deliberation and Suppressed Voices *21*
The Public Sphere and Appropriate Heterogeneity *23*

NOTES   27

ABOUT THE AUTHOR   29

Acknowledgments

I am grateful to many people for help with this manuscript. Special thanks to Robert Hahn and Christopher DeMuth for inviting me to speak on this subject, and for an energetic and spirited discussion and dinner, which provided a great deal of help. For relevant discussions and comments, thanks to Martha Nussbaum, Eric Posner, Richard Posner, and Adrian Vermeule. I have also adapted some material from Cass R. Sunstein, *Why Societies Need Dissent* (Harvard University Press, 2003), and Cass R. Sunstein, *Deliberative Trouble?* (Yale Law Journal, 2000), though I have significantly revised some of the discussion here.

Foreword

The 2007 AEI Center for Regulatory and Market Studies Distinguished Lecture Award was given to Professor Cass Sunstein. The purpose of the award is to recognize a person who has made major contributions to the field of regulation and related areas. Senior members of the Reg-Markets Center select the distinguished lecturer on the basis of scholarly and practical contributions to the field. The lecturer is given complete latitude in choosing a topic for the lecture.

Professor Sunstein is one of the leading law professors of his generation. He is one of those rare individuals who has the ability to develop new insights and synthesize knowledge across a wide range of subject areas. His scholarship spans the fields of psychology, economics, politics, philosophy, and law. He has been a leading contributor and supporter of the Reg-Markets Center and, before that, the AEI-Brookings Joint Center for Regulatory Studies.

His work on benefit-cost analysis has been particularly important in fostering a more enlightened dialogue on this important subject. He has tackled a number of issues that are of critical importance to policymakers, including the treatment of uncertainty, ways of addressing irreversibility, and the design of institutions for making better regulatory decisions. His broad contributions in this area have had an important impact on how benefit-cost analysis is used throughout the world.

In this monograph, Professor Sunstein focuses on the issue of decision-making in groups. He uses recent studies of juries, federal judges, and ordinary citizens to show that groups of like-minded people often move to extreme positions on many questions, including climate change, labor policy, same-sex relationships, and affirmative action. This "ideological amplification" helps to explain phenomena like punitive damage awards, excessive and insufficient regulation, political correctness, ethnic conflict, and even terrorism. Professor Sunstein suggests how techniques such as benefit-cost analysis can be used to help address extremism and its consequences.

Like all Reg-Markets Center publications, this monograph can be freely downloaded at www.reg-markets.org. We encourage educators to use and distribute these materials to their students.

ROBERT HAHN, *Executive Director,*
AEI Center for Regulatory and Market Studies

Why Groups Go to Extremes
Cass R. Sunstein

The Basic Phenomenon

Much of the time, groups of people end up doing things that group members would never do on their own. This is true for groups of teenagers, who take risks that individuals would avoid. It is true for student organizations, labor unions, political protestors, police officers, and juries. It is certainly true for those prone to violence, including terrorists.

In order to understand why this is so, we need to explore the phenomenon of *group polarization*, which offers large lessons about the behavior of interest groups, religious organizations, political parties, executive agencies, legislatures, judicial panels, and even nations.

What happens within deliberating bodies? Do groups compromise? Do they move toward the middle of the tendencies of their individual members? The answer is now clear, and it is not what intuition would suggest: *members of a deliberating group usually end up at a more extreme position in the same general direction as their inclinations before deliberation began.*[1] This is the phenomenon known as group polarization. Group polarization is the typical pattern with deliberating groups. It has been found in hundreds of studies involving over a dozen countries, including the United States, France, Afghanistan, and Germany.[2]

Consider a few examples:

1. Those who approve of an ongoing war effort will, as a result of discussion, become still more enthusiastic about that effort.

2. People who dislike the head of state, and his current tendencies, will dislike him more intensely after talking with one another.

3. Those who disapprove of the United States, and are suspicious of its intentions, will increase their disapproval and suspicion if they exchange points of view. Indeed, there is specific evidence of the latter phenomenon among citizens of France.[3]

4. White people who tend to show significant racial prejudice will show more racial prejudice after speaking with one another; white people who tend to show little racial prejudice will show less racial prejudice after speaking with one another.[4]

In these and countless other cases, like-minded people tend, after discussions with one another, to end up thinking a more extreme version of what they thought before they started to talk. It should be readily apparent that enclaves of people, separated from others and inclined to rebellion or even violence, might move sharply in that direction as a consequence of internal deliberations. Political extremism is often a product of group polarization.[5] In fact, a good way to create an extremist group, or a cult of any kind, is to separate members from the rest of society, either physically or psychologically, by creating a sense of suspicion about nonmembers. With either form of separation, the information and views of those outside the group can be discredited, and hence nothing need disturb the process of polarization as group members continue to talk.

I have been involved in three sets of investigations of group polarization, involving citizens, judges, and juries. To understand the nature of the basic phenomenon and its range and generality, let me outline the central findings here.

Citizens

A small experiment in democracy was held in Colorado in 2005.[6] About sixty American citizens were brought together and assembled into ten groups, most of them consisting of six people. Members of each group were asked to deliberate on three of the most controversial issues of the day. *Should states allow same-sex couples to enter into civil unions? Should employers engage in "affirmative action" by giving a preference to members of traditionally disadvantaged groups? Should the United States sign an international treaty to combat global warming?*

As the experiment was designed, the groups consisted of "liberal" and "conservative" members—the former from Boulder, the latter from Colorado Springs. It is widely known that Boulder tends to be liberal and that Colorado Springs tends to be conservative. The groups were screened to ensure that their members generally conformed to these stereotypes. For example, group members were asked to report on their assessment of Vice President Cheney. In Boulder, those who liked him were excused from the experiment; in Colorado Springs, those who disliked him were similarly excused.

In the parlance of election years, the experiment created five "Blue State" groups, whose members tended toward liberal positions in general, and five "Red State" groups, whose members tended toward conservative positions. On the three issues, however, participants were not screened at all. They were asked to state their opinions anonymously both before and after fifteen minutes of group discussion, and also to try to reach a public verdict before the final anonymous statement. As the experiment was designed, participants followed norms of civic respect; the tapes of the discussions reveal that for most of the participants, there was an effort to think hard, to listen to others, and to be reasonable. What was the effect of discussion?

The results were simple. In almost every group, members ended up with more extreme positions after they spoke with one another. Liberals favored an international treaty to control global warming before discussion; they favored it more strongly after discussion. Conservatives were neutral on that treaty before discussion; they strongly opposed it after discussion. Discussion made civil unions more popular among liberals; discussion made civil unions less popular among conservatives. Mildly favorable toward affirmative action before discussion, liberals became strongly favorable toward affirmative action after discussion. Firmly negative about affirmative action before discussion, conservatives became even more negative about affirmative action after discussion.

Aside from increasing extremism, the experiment had an independent effect, one that is equally important: *it made both liberal groups and conservative groups significantly more homogeneous—and thus squelched diversity.* Before members started to talk, many groups displayed a fair bit of internal disagreement. The disagreements were reduced as a result of a mere fifteen-minute discussion. Note that my primary test here involves comparing members' anonymous statements before and after deliberation. Group members showed far more consensus after discussion than before.

It follows that discussion helped to widen the rift between liberals and conservatives on all three issues. Before discussion, some liberal groups were, on some issues, fairly close to some conservative groups. The result of discussion was to divide them far more sharply.

Federal Judges and Polarized Differences

Over the past decades, the United States has been conducting a truly extraordinary natural experiment. On federal courts of appeals, judicial panels consist of three judges. The possible panel compositions are just four: (a) three Republican appointees; (b) three Democratic appointees; (c) two Republican appointees and one Democratic appointee; and (d) two Democratic appointees and one Republican appointee. Because panel assignments are random, and because the sample is so large, it is possible to test whether judicial votes are affected by panel composition—that is, whether Republican and Democratic appointees vote differently depending on whether they are sitting with other Republican appointees or with one or two Democratic appointees.

For present purposes, the key questions are these: how do Republican appointees vote on panels consisting solely of Republican appointees (RRR panels), and how do Democratic appointees vote on panels consisting solely of Democratic appointees (DDD panels)? RRR panels are a bit like Colorado Springs and DDD panels are a bit like Boulder; do federal judges behave like participants in the Colorado experiment? More specifically, we might ask whether Rs, on RRR panels, behave differently from Rs on RRD panels or RDD panels, and whether Ds, on DDD panels, behave differently from Ds on DDR or DRR panels.

The phenomenon of group polarization suggests a simple hypothesis. Wherever Ds and Rs show a general difference in voting patterns, that difference will be *amplified* if we compare Ds on DDD panels to Rs on RRR panels. That is, the aggregate or overall difference between the liberal voting rates of Ds and the liberal voting rates of Rs should be smaller than the difference between the liberal voting rates of Ds on DDD panels and the liberal voting rates of Rs on RRR panels. The latter difference—between Ds on DDD panels and Rs or RRR panels— might be called the *polarized difference*. In countless areas, this is exactly the pattern we observe. Democratic appointees show especially liberal voting patterns on DDD panels. Republican appointees show especially conservative voting patterns on RRR panels. If we aggregate all cases showing an ideological difference, we find a 15 percent difference between Republican and Democratic appointees in liberal voting rates. But the polarized difference is far higher—34 percent!

Our method was quite simple. We collected tens of thousands of judicial votes, mostly in ideologically contested cases, which involved issues such as race discrimination, sex discrimination, environmental protection, labor, and free speech. We used simple, relatively uncontroversial tests to code decisions as "liberal" or "conservative." For example, a decision in favor of an African-American plaintiff alleging race discrimination was coded as liberal, as was a vote to uphold an affirmative action program, a campaign finance restriction, an environmental regulation challenged as too aggressive, or a decision of the National Labor Relations Board (NLRB) in favor of employees. These tests of whether a judicial decision is "liberal" are admittedly crude, but because of the large size of the sample, we were nonetheless able to discern clear and illuminating patterns, and the crudeness of the tests does not seem to have introduced distortions.

Consider a few examples.[7]

- In gay rights cases, the overall spread between Rs and Ds is 41 percent— Rs vote in favor of gay rights 16 percent of the time, compared to a 57 percent rate for Ds. But if we compare how Ds vote on DDD panels to how Rs vote on RRR panels, the polarized difference turns out to be more than double—86 percent (14 percent in favor of gay rights for Rs on RRR panels, compared to 100 percent for Ds on DDD panels).

- In cases involving the National Environmental Policy Act, the difference in liberal voting rates is a substantial 24 percent; but the polarized difference is much greater, 51 percent.

- In affirmative action cases, the difference is a significant 28 percent; the polarized difference is a whopping 49 percent.

- In sex discrimination cases, the overall difference is 17 percent; the polarized difference is 46 percent.

- In Americans with Disabilities Act cases, the overall difference is 16 percent, but the polarized difference is twice as great, at 33 percent.

- In campaign finance cases, the overall difference is 14 percent, but the polarized difference is more than double, at 31 percent.

The general pattern holds in cases in which courts review regulatory decisions by the Environmental Protection Agency (EPA) and the National Labor Relations Board. Some of the most important regulatory cases involve "arbitrariness" and "substantial evidence" review;

these are cases in which courts ask whether an agency's judgments of policy and fact are essentially reasonable. In cases reviewing decisions of the EPA and the NLRB, Republican appointees vote in a stereotypically liberal way 56 percent of the time, a rate significantly lower than the Democratic rate of 68 percent. But this 12 percentage point difference jumps to a 22 percent polarized difference between RRR and DDD panels.[8]

Juries

Now let me turn to jury behavior, and in particular to the effects of deliberation on punitive damage awards. Such awards are of considerable importance in their own right. Companies are greatly concerned about unpredictable and sometimes very high awards, in the hundreds of millions of dollars; many efforts have been made to discipline jury decisions, and the Supreme Court has taken an active interest in the problem. In addition, punitive damage awards provide an excellent area in which to study the consequences of discussion, especially for people who display a degree of outrage— and because of its importance to extremism, outrage is one of my central concerns here.

To see those consequences, we must begin with a study of individuals, not groups, involving about a thousand people, who were asked to register their judgments about misconduct by a corporate defendant.[9] The judgments were elicited on three scales: the unbounded scale of dollars; a bounded scale of 0 to 8, involving outrage; and a bounded scale of 0 to 8, involving appropriate punishment (on both scales, 8 means "extremely severe" and 0 means "none"). The goal was to understand why punitive damage awards have a high degree of variability. The central findings, involving personal injury cases, were as follows. When individual responses are pooled to produce "statistical juries," whose verdict is the judgment of the median member, we find that small groups of people—or statistical juries, established through the magic of the computer—will agree about two things. First, they will agree about the appropriate degree of outrage on the bounded scale of 0–8. Second, they will agree about the appropriate punishment, also on the bounded scale—at least, in both cases, if the points on the scale are labeled. The agreement cuts across demographic differences. With the help of the computer, we can create statistical juries of any imaginable kind—all male, all female, all white, all Hispanic, all African-American, all rich, all poor, all old, all young, all well-educated, all poorly educated. Demography does not matter. Remarkably, all these groups essentially agree with one another about how outrageous the act in question is, and how severely it deserves to be punished.

By contrast, statistical juries show a high degree of variability with respect to dollar awards. The dollar judgment of one jury is not a good predictor of the dollar judgment of other juries. Demography is not the source of the variability; the problem is the dollar scale. Whatever their demographic group, people do not have a clear sense of how to translate their punitive intentions, on a bounded scale, into the scale of dollars. The problem is that the dollar scale, bounded at the lower end ($0) and essentially unbounded at the upper end, lacks signposts that give meaning to the various "points" on the scale. For this reason, people who agree that the case is a 6 on a scale of 0–8 may not agree on the appropriate translation of that figure into some monetary equivalent. Does a 6 mean a punishment of $50,000, or $100,000, or $1 million, or $10 million, or more? People do not know. Note that the variability, or noise, in the judgments of statistical juries cannot be attributed to people's demographic characteristics. It is not as if rich people disagree with poor people, or old with young, or white with African-American. The problem is the dollar scale, which simply produces a lot of noise.

The study I have just described involved an effort to pool individual responses; it did not involve group deliberation. If we want to understand how juries actually behave, this is a serious defect. A follow-up experiment, involving about three thousand jury-eligible citizens and five hundred deliberating juries (of six people each), was designed to determine how individuals would be influenced by seeing and discussing the views of others.[10] Here is how the experiment worked. People read about a personal injury case, including the arguments made by both sides. They were also asked to record, in advance of deliberation, an individual "punishment judgment" on a bounded scale of 0 to 8, where (again) 0 indicated that the defendant should not be punished at all, and 8 indicated that the defendant should be punished extremely severely. After the individual judgments were recorded, jurors were sorted into six-person groups and asked to deliberate to a unanimous "punishment verdict." It would be reasonable to predict that people would compromise and hence that the verdicts of juries would be the median of punishment judgments of jurors. But this prediction would be badly wrong.

Instead, the effect of deliberation was to create both a *severity shift* for high-punishment jurors and a *leniency shift* for low-punishment jurors. When the median judgment of individual jurors was 4 or higher on the 8-point scale, the jury's verdict was above that median judgment. Consider, for example, a case involving a man who nearly drowned on a defectively constructed yacht. Jurors tended to be outraged by the idea of a defectively built yacht, and groups were significantly more outraged than their median members. High levels of outrage, and severe punitive judgments, became higher and more severe as a result of group interactions. But when the median judgment of individual jurors was below 4, the jury's verdict was typically below that median judgment. Consider a case involving a shopper who was injured in a fall when an escalator suddenly stopped. Individual jurors were not greatly bothered by the incident, seeing it as a genuine accident rather than a case of serious wrongdoing. Juries were more lenient than individual jurors.

With dollar awards, by contrast, juries were systematically more severe in their awards than the median juror. Even the small awards were typically higher than the predeliberation award selected by the median juror. Here is the most striking finding: *in 27 percent of the cases, the jury's award was at least as high as that of the highest predeliberation judgment of the members of that particular jury!* In this study, we did not record anonymous postdeliberation judgments, so it is not possible to offer a clean comparison with the predeliberation and postdeliberation shifts in Colorado. But in most experiments, people's anonymous postdeliberation statements tend to be generally in line with public commitments to unanimous verdicts, and there is every reason to suspect that the severity shift, with respect to outrage and dollar awards, would be replicated in anonymous statements as well.

In any case, what is important for jury awards is the group's judgment, not the anonymous judgments of group members. The key finding is that in producing monetary awards, juries are significantly more extreme than jurors.

Why Polarization? Some Explanations

Why do like-minded people go to extremes? There are several reasons.[11]

Information Strengthens Antecedent Beliefs. The most important reason involves information. People tend to respond to the arguments made by other people—and the "argument pool," in any group with some predisposition in one direction, will inevitably be skewed toward that predisposition. A group whose members tend to think that Israel is the real aggressor in the Mideast conflict, or that same-sex unions are a good idea, or that the minimum wage should be increased, will hear many arguments to that effect. Because of the initial distribution of views, members of that same group will hear relatively fewer opposing views. It is inevitable that the group members will have heard some, but not all, of the arguments that emerge from the discussion. After they have heard all of what is said, there is likely to be further movement in the anti-Israel or pro–same-sex-union direction.

So too with a group whose members tend to oppose affirmative action. Group members will hear a number of arguments against affirmative action and fewer arguments on its behalf. If people are listening, they will have a stronger conviction, in the same direction from which they began, as a result of deliberation.

Corroboration Breeds Confidence, Which Breeds Extremism. The second explanation begins by noting that those who lack confidence, and who are unsure what they should think, tend to moderate their views.[12] It is for this reason that cautious people, not knowing what to do, are likely to choose the midpoint between relevant extremes.[13] But if other people seem to share their views, people are likely to become more confident that they are correct. As a result, they will probably move at least slightly in a more extreme direction.

In a wide variety of experimental contexts, people's opinions have been shown to become more extreme simply because their view has been corroborated, and because they grow more confident after learning of the shared views of others.[14] Note that there is an obvious connection between this explanation and the finding that Republican appointees on a panel of three Republican appointees are likely to be more extreme than Republican appointees on a panel with only two such judges. The existence of unanimous confirmation, from two others, will strengthen confidence—and hence strengthen extremity (here defined in terms of voting patterns).[15]

What is especially noteworthy here is that this process—of increased confidence and increased extremism—might well be occurring simultaneously for all participants. Suppose that a group of four people is inclined to distrust the intentions of the United States with respect to foreign aid. Seeing her tentative view confirmed by three others, each member is likely to feel vindicated, to hold her view more confidently, and to move in a more extreme direction. Simultaneously, the very same internal movements are also occurring in *other* people (from corroboration to more confidence, and from more confidence to more extremism). But those movements will not be highly visible to each participant. It will simply appear as if others "really" hold their views without hesitation. As a result, our little group might conclude after a day's discussion that the intentions of the United States, with respect to foreign aid, cannot be trusted at all.

Social Comparisons Shift Positions. A third explanation, involving social comparison, begins with the claim that people want to be perceived favorably by other group members, and also to perceive themselves favorably. Sometimes our views are, to a greater or lesser extent, a function of how we want to present ourselves. Once we hear what others believe, some of us will adjust our positions at least slightly in the direction of the dominant position, to hold onto our preferred self-presentation.

Some people might want to show, for example, that they are not cowardly or cautious, especially in an entrepreneurial group that disparages these characteristics. Hence they will frame their position so that they do not appear cowardly or cautious by comparison to other group members. And when they hear what other people think, they might find that they occupy a somewhat different position, in relation to the group, from what they hoped; and they shift accordingly.[16] This might be because they want others to see them in a certain way. Or it might be because they want to see themselves in a certain way.

Suppose, for example, that the group members believe that they are somewhat more opposed to capital punishment than are most people. Such people might shift a bit after finding themselves in a group of people who are strongly opposed to capital punishment, simply to maintain their preferred self-presentation. Does the example seem unrealistic? Consider the otherwise inexplicably extreme behavior of many Republicans and many Democrats in the debate over the presidential vote in Florida in 2000. Reasonable people could differ at the time. Each side had something to say. But many members of both parties, talking and listening mostly to one another, shifted to ludicrously extreme positions, suggesting that the other party was trying to steal the election. The phenomenon occurs in many contexts. People might wish not to seem too enthusiastic about, or too restrained in their enthusiasm for, a particular political candidate, a response to a national security threat, affirmative action, feminism, or an increase in national defense; hence their views shift when they see what other group members think. The result is to press the group's position toward one or another extreme, and also to induce shifts in individual members.

Polarization and Democracy

In this section I discuss evidence of group polarization in legal and political institutions, and I trace some implications of that evidence for participants in a deliberative democracy. I will deal with normative issues below; my purpose here is to cast a new light on social practices.

Polarizing Events and Polarization Entrepreneurs. Group polarization has a large effect on many deliberating groups and institutions. Consider, for example, the political and social role of religious organizations. Such organizations tend to strengthen group members' religious convictions, simply by virtue of the fact that they encourage like-minded people to talk to one another. Religious groups amplify the religious impulse, especially if group members are insulated from other groups. Moreover, political activity by members of religious organizations is undoubtedly affected by cascade-like effects and by group polarization. In a related vein, survey evidence shows that dramatic social events, like the assassination of Martin Luther King and civil rights disturbances, tend to polarize attitudes, with both positive and negative attitudes increasing within demographic groups.[17] The point emphatically holds for the terrorist attacks in New York City and Washington, D.C., on September 11, 2001.

In fact it is possible to imagine "professional polarizers," or "polarization entrepreneurs," that is, political activists who have, as one of their goals, the creation of spheres in which like-minded people can hear a particular point of view from one or more articulate people, and also participate, actually or vicariously, in a deliberative discussion in which a certain point of view becomes entrenched and strengthened. For those seeking to promote social reform, an extremely promising strategy is to begin by promoting discussions among people who tend to favor the relevant reform; such discussions are likely to intensify the underlying convictions and concerns. Social reformers of all stripes may qualify as polarization entrepreneurs; the category includes those fighting communism in Eastern Europe and apartheid in South Africa, as well as terrorist leaders and those involved in criminal conspiracies of many kinds.

Outgroups. Group polarization has particular implications for understanding the nature of insulated outgroups and (in the extreme case) both conspiracies and conspiracy theorists. Polarization increases when group members identify themselves along some salient dimension, and especially when the group is able to define itself by contrast to another group. Outgroups are in this position—of self-contrast to others—by definition. Excluded by choice or coercion from discussion with others, such groups may become polarized in quite extreme directions, often in part because of group polarization. It is for this reason that outgroup members can sometimes be led, or lead themselves, to odd beliefs and even to violent acts.

The tendency toward polarization among outgroups helps explain special concern about "hate speech," which can heighten group antagonisms, and it simultaneously raises some questions about the idea that certain group discussions produce "consciousness raising." It is possible, at least, that the consequence of discussion is not only or mostly to raise consciousness (an ambiguous idea to be sure), but to produce group polarization in one direction or another—and at the same time to increase confidence in the position that has newly emerged. This does not mean that consciousness is never raised; undoubtedly group discussion can identify and clarify problems that were previously repressed, or understood as an individual rather than social product. But the mere fact that views have changed and coalesced, and are held, post-discussion, with a high degree of confidence, does not establish that consciousness has been raised.

Feuds, Ethnic and International Strife, and War. Group polarization is inevitably at work in feuds, ethnic and international strife, and war. One of the characteristic features of feuds is that members of feuding groups tend to talk only to one another, fueling and amplifying their outrage, and solidifying their impression of the relevant events. Informational and reputational forces are very much at work here, producing cascade effects, and group polarization can lead members to increasingly extreme positions. It is not too much of a leap to suggest that these effects are sometimes present within ethnic groups and even nations, notwithstanding the usually high degree of national heterogeneity. In the United States, occasionally sharp divergences between whites and African-Americans, on particular salient events or more generally, can be explained by reference to group polarization. The same is true for sharp divergences of viewpoints within and across nations. Group polarization occurs within Israel and as well as within the Palestinian Authority; it occurs within the United States and among those inclined to support, or at least not to condemn, terrorist acts.

When members of some nations conclude that the 9/11 attack was plotted by the United States or Israel, or that the United States is responsible for all or most evils in the world, polarization entrepreneurs and group polarization play a significant role. A large part of the answer to the perennial question, "Why do they hate us?" lies not in ancient grievances or individual consciences, but in the influences of social processes emphasized here. Of course the media play a large role, as we shall now see.

The Internet, Communications Policy, and Mass Deliberation.
Many people have expressed concern about processes of social influence on the mass media and the Internet. The general problem is said to be one of fragmentation, with certain people hearing more and louder versions of their own preexisting commitments, thus reducing the benefits that come from exposure to competing views and unnoticed problems. With greater specialization, people are increasingly able to avoid general interest newspapers and magazines, and to make choices that reflect their own predispositions. The Internet is making it possible for people to design their own highly individuated communications packages, filtering out troublesome issues and disfavored voices. Long before the Internet, it was possible to discuss the "racial stratification of the public sphere" by reference to divergences between white and African-American newspapers.[18] New communications technologies may increase this phenomenon.

An understanding of group polarization explains why a fragmented communications market may create problems.[19] A "plausible hypothesis is that the Internet-like setting is most likely to create a strong tendency toward group polarization when the members of the group feel some sense of group identity."[20] If certain people are deliberating with many like-minded others, views will not be reinforced but instead shifted to more extreme points. This cannot be said to be bad by itself—perhaps the increased extremism is good—but it is certainly troublesome if diverse social groups are led, through predictable mechanisms, toward increasingly opposing and ever more extreme views.

Deliberative Trouble

I now turn to normative issues, involving the relationship among group polarization, democratic theory, and legal institutions. I focus in particular on the implications of group polarization for institutional design, with special reference to the uses of heterogeneity and the complex issues presented by deliberation inside particular enclaves. Let us consider, then, the problem of *enclave deliberation*— deliberation within enclaves of like-minded people.

The initial question is simple: Should enclave deliberation count as deliberation at all? If deliberation requires a measure of disagreement, this is a serious question. But even like-minded people usually have different perspectives and views, so that discussion by a group of people who tend to favor some military undertaking, or to fear global warming, will still involve some kind of exchange of opinion. I will urge that in spite of its many advantages and virtues, enclave deliberation sometimes raises serious difficulties for the participants and possibly for society as a whole. But there are many complexities here. In some cases, enclave deliberation will be a defective form for the participants, but will serve to foster a diversity of views for the wider public, and will therefore be desirable from the social point of view.

The central problem is that widespread error and social fragmentation are likely to result when like-minded people, insulated from others, move in extreme directions simply because of limited argument pools and parochial influences. As an extreme example, consider a system of one-party domination, which stifles dissent in part because it refuses to establish space for the emergence of divergent positions; in this way, it intensifies polarization within the party while also disabling external criticism. In terms of institutional design, the most natural response is to try to ensure that members of deliberating groups, whether small or large, will not isolate themselves from competing views. This point has many implications for multimember courts, open primaries, freedom of association, and the architecture of the Internet. Here, then, is a plea for ensuring that deliberation occurs not only in enclaves but also in a large and heterogeneous public sphere, and for guarding against a situation in which like-minded people wall themselves off from alternative perspectives.

But there is a qualification to this response: a certain measure of isolation will, in some cases, be crucial to the development of ideas and approaches that would not otherwise emerge and that deserve a social hearing. Members of low-status groups are often quiet within heterogeneous bodies, and thus deliberation in such bodies tends to be dominated by high-status members. In many groups, men speak more than women, and men are listened to more carefully as well. Any shift—in technology, norms, or legal practice—that increases the number of deliberating enclaves will increase the diversity of society's aggregate argument pool while also increasing the danger of extremism and instability, and ultimately even violence. Terrorism itself is a product, in part, of group polarization. At the same time, shifts toward a general "public sphere," without much in the way of enclave deliberation, will decrease the likelihood of extremism and instability, but at the same time produce what may be a stifling uniformity.

No algorithm is available to solve the resulting conundrums. But some general lessons do emerge. It is important to ensure social spaces for deliberation by like-minded persons, but it is equally important to ensure that members of the relevant groups are not isolated from conversation with people having quite different views. The goal of that conversation is to promote the interests of those inside and outside the relevant enclaves by subjecting group members to competing positions, by allowing them to exchange views with others and to see things from their point of view, and by ensuring that the wider society does not marginalize, and thus insulate itself from, views that may turn out to be right or at least informative.

Why Deliberate?

If the effect of deliberation is to move people toward a more extreme point in the direction of their original tendency, why is deliberation anything to celebrate? The discussion thus far does not provide much reason for confidence in the outcome of deliberation. If people are shifting their position in order to maintain their reputation and self-conception within groups that may or may not be representative of the public as a whole, is there any reason to think that deliberation is making things better rather than worse? To the extent that shifts are occurring as a result of partial and frequently skewed argument pools, the results of deliberative judgments may be far worse than the results of simply taking the median of predeliberation judgments.

The most important point here is that those who emphasize the ideals associated with deliberative democracy tend to emphasize its preconditions, which include political equality, an absence of strategic behavior, full information, and the goal of "reaching understanding."[21] In real-world deliberations, behavior is often strategic, and equality is often absent in one or another form. But the existence of a limited argument pool, strengthening the existing tendency within the group, will operate to promote group polarization even if no individual behaves strategically. By itself this will produce group polarization whether or not social influence is operating. On the other hand, the social context of deliberation can make a large difference, and it suggests that under certain conditions, group polarization need not occur. The nature of the deliberative process, and the characteristics of the deliberating participants, can matter a great deal. I will return to this issue below.

In any case, social influences need not be inconsistent with the effort to produce truth and understanding; when people attempt to position themselves in a way that fits with their best self-conception, or their preferred self-presentation, nothing has necessarily gone wrong, even from the standpoint of deliberation's most enthusiastic defenders. Perhaps group polarization could be reduced or even eliminated if we emphasized that good deliberation has full information as a precondition; by hypothesis, argument pools would not be limited if all information were available. But that requirement is extremely stringent, and if there is already full information, the need for deliberation is greatly reduced. The general point is that the phenomenon of group polarization suggests that in real-world situations, deliberation is hardly guaranteed to increase the likelihood of arriving at truth. The trick is to produce an institutional design that will increase the likelihood that deliberation will lead in sensible directions, so that any polarization, if it occurs, will be a result of learning, rather than group dynamics.

Of course we cannot say, from the mere fact of polarization, that there has been a movement in the wrong direction. Perhaps the more extreme tendency is better; group polarization is likely to have fueled the antislavery movement, the downfall of communism, the civil rights movement, and many other movements that deserve widespread approval. In the context of punitive damage awards, perhaps a severity shift produces good outcomes. Extremism should hardly be a word of opprobrium; everything depends on what extremists are arguing *for*. But when group discussion tends to lead people to more strongly held versions of the same view with which they began, and when social influences and limited argument pools are responsible, there is little reason for great confidence in the effects of deliberation.

We can go further. Some points of view are unreasonable and even potentially dangerous, and it is also possible to worry about group discussion among people who share such points of view. If the underlying views are unreasonable, it makes sense to fear that these discussions may fuel increasing hatred and extremism (used here in an evaluative sense). This does not mean that the discussions can or should be regulated in a system dedicated to freedom of speech. But it does raise questions about the idea that "more speech" is necessarily an adequate remedy.

The Virtues of Heterogeneity

The simplest lesson here involves both individual susceptibility and institutional design. For many people, mere awareness of the role of limited argument pools and social influences might provide some inoculation against inadequately justified movements of opinion within groups. (Leaders of public and private institutions should take note; good institutions frequently get in bad trouble because leaders ignore this risk.) More important, institutions might well be designed to ensure that when shifts are occurring, it is not because of arbitrary or illegitimate constraints on the available range of arguments. In the public sphere, this is a central task of constitutional design, and in this light a system of checks and balances might be viewed not as an undemocratic check on the will of the people, but as an effort to protect against potentially harmful consequences of group discussion by like-minded types.

To explore some of the advantages of heterogeneity, imagine a deliberating body consisting of all citizens in the relevant group; this may mean all citizens in a community, a state, a nation, or the world. By hypothesis, the argument pool would be very large. It would be limited only to the extent that the set of citizen views was similarly limited. Social influences would undoubtedly remain. Hence people might shift because of a desire to maintain their reputation and self-conception in relation to the rest of the group. But to the extent that deliberation revealed to people that their private position was different, in relation to the group, from what they thought it was, any shift would be in response to an accurate understanding of all relevant citizens, and not a product of a skewed group sample.

This thought experiment does not suggest that the hypothesized deliberating body would be ideal. Perhaps weak arguments would be made and repeated and repeated again, while good arguments would be offered infrequently. In a pervasively unjust society, a deliberating body consisting of everyone may produce nothing to celebrate. (As we will see below, it is often important to ensure the existence of enclaves in which polarization will take place, precisely in order to ensure the emergence of views that are suppressed, by social influences or otherwise, but that are reasonable or even right.) But at least a deliberating body of all citizens would remove some of the distortions in the group polarization experiments, where generally like-minded people, not exposed to others, shift in large part because of that limited exposure. Hence the outcomes of these deliberations will not be a product of the arbitrariness that can be introduced by skewed argument pools.

Enclave Deliberation and Suppressed Voices

Let us now consider the potential vices of heterogeneity and the potentially desirable effects of deliberating enclaves, consisting of groups of like-minded individuals. It seems obvious that such groups can be extremely important in a heterogeneous society, not least because members of some demographic groups tend to be especially quiet when participating in broader deliberative bodies. In this light, a special advantage of enclave deliberation is that it promotes the development of positions that would otherwise be invisible, silenced, or squelched in general debate. While this is literally dangerous in numerous contexts, it can also be a great advantage; many desirable social movements have been made possible through this route. The efforts of marginalized groups to exclude outsiders, and even of political parties to limit their primaries to party members, can be justified in similar terms. Even if group polarization is at work— indeed *because* group polarization is at work—enclaves can pro- vide a wide range of social benefits, not least because they greatly enrich the social argument pool. In the academic sphere, we can see this phenomenon in the rise of "schools" of various sorts, such as the Chicago School of economics. In the political sphere, the existence of religious groups, libertarian groups, conservative think tanks, and liberal think tanks has added many valuable arguments to the public domain.

A central empirical point here is that in deliberating bodies, high-status members tend to initiate communication more than others, and their ideas are more influential, partly because low- status members lack confidence in their own abilities, partly because they fear retribution.[22] For example, women's ideas are often less influential and sometimes are "suppressed altogether in mixed-gender groups,"[23] and in ordinary circumstances, cultural minorities have disproportionately little influence on decisions by cultural mixed groups.[24] In some groups, liberal perspectives are squelched as "politically incorrect"; in other groups, conservative perspectives are squelched on the same ground. Interestingly, there is evidence that with changes in gender norms, men and women are now equally influential in some situations, a finding that confirms the claim that people's role in group deliberation will be influenced by whether social norms produce status hierarchies. In these circumstances, it makes sense to promote deliberating enclaves in which members of multiple groups may speak with one another and develop their views.

But there is a serious danger in such enclaves. The danger is that through the mechanisms of social influence and persuasive arguments, members will move to positions that lack merit but are predictable consequences of the particular circumstances of enclave deliberation—as, for example, in the rise of terrorist organizations and cults of many diverse kinds. In the extreme case, enclave deliberation may even put social stability at risk (sometimes for better, usually for worse). And it is impossible to say, in the abstract, that those who sort themselves into enclaves will generally move in a direction that is desirable for society at large or even for enclave members themselves.

There is no simple solution to the dangers of enclave deliberation. Sometimes the threat to social stability is desirable. From the standpoint of institutional design, the problem is that any effort to promote enclave deliberation will ensure group polarization among a wide range of groups, some necessary to the pursuit of sense or justice, others likely to promote senselessness or injustice, and some potentially quite dangerous. In this light we should be able to see more clearly the sense in which Edmund Burke's conception of representation—rejecting "local purposes" and "local prejudices" in favor of "the general reason of the whole"[25]—is not contingently but is instead *essentially* conservative (speaking purely descriptively, as a safeguard of existing practices). The reason is that the submersion of "local purposes" and "local prejudices" into a heterogeneous "deliberative assembly" will inevitably tend to weaken the resolve of groups—and particularly low-status or marginalized groups—whose purely internal deliberations would produce a high degree of polarization.

Hence James Madison—with his fear of popular passions producing "a rage for paper money, for an abolition of debts, for an equal division of property, or for any other improper or wicked project"[26]—would naturally be drawn to a Burkean conception of representation, favoring large election districts and long length of service to counteract the forces of passion or polarization.[27] By contrast, those who believe that "destabilization" is an intrinsic good, or that the irrationality or unfairness of the status quo justifies the risks of encouraging polarization on the part of diverse groups, will, or should, be drawn to a system that enthusiastically promotes insular deliberation within enclaves.

In a nation in which most people are confused or evil, enclave deliberation may be the only way to develop a sense of clarity or justice, at least for some. But even in such a nation, enclave deliberation is unlikely to produce change unless its members are eventually brought into contact with others. In democratic societies, the best response is to ensure that any such enclaves are not walled off from competing views, and that at certain points there is an exchange of views between enclave members and those who disagree with them. It is total or near-total self-insulation, rather than group deliberation as such, that carries with it the most serious dangers, often in the highly unfortunate (and sometimes deadly) combination of extremism with marginality.

The Public Sphere and Appropriate Heterogeneity

A reasonable conclusion would return to the need for full information, not only about facts but also about relevant values and options, and suggest that for a designer or leader of any institution, it makes sense to promote ample social space both for enclave deliberation and for discussions involving a broad array of views, including the views of those who have been within enclaves. The idea of a "public sphere," developed most prominently by Jürgen Habermas, can be understood as part of an effort to ensure a domain in which multiple views can be heard by people with multiple perspectives.[28] Of course any argument pool will be limited. No one has time to listen to every point of view. But an understanding of group polarization helps show that heterogeneous groups are often a far better source of good judgments, simply because more arguments will be made available.

The point very much bears on the continuing debate over proportional or group representation.[29] On one approach, political groups should be allowed to have representation to the extent that they are able to get more than a minimal share of the vote. On another approach, steps would be taken to increase the likelihood that members of disadvantaged or marginal groups—perhaps African-Americans, religious minorities, gays and lesbians, women—would have their own representatives in the deliberating body. The decision whether to move in one or another direction depends on many factors, and an understanding of group polarization is hardly sufficient. But at least it can be said that proportional or group representation draws strength from the goal of ensuring exposure to a diverse range of views.

One advantage of group representation is that it might help counteract the risks of polarization that come from deliberation among like-minded people. At the same time, group representation should help reduce the dangers that come from insulation of those in the smaller enclave, by subjecting enclave representations to a broader debate. For these purposes, it might well be insufficient that representatives, not themselves members of any enclave, are electorally accountable to constituents who include enclave members. The point of group representation is to promote a process in which those who are actually in the enclave hear what others have to say, and in which those in other enclaves, or in no enclave at all, are able to listen to people with very different points of view.

The principal qualification here is that the real question is how to ensure *appropriate* heterogeneity. For example, it would not make sense to say that in a deliberating group attempting to think through issues of affirmative action, it is important to allow exposure to people who think that slavery was good and should be restored. The constraints of time and attention call for limits to heterogeneity; and—a separate point—in order for good deliberation to take place, some views are properly placed off the table, simply because time is limited and they are so invidious, implausible, or both. This point seems to create a final conundrum: to know what points of view should be represented in any group deliberation, it is important to have a good sense of the substantive issues involved, indeed a sufficiently good sense as to generate judgments about what points of view must be included and excluded. But if we already know that, why should we not proceed directly to the merits? If we already know that, before deliberation occurs, does deliberation have any point at all?

The answer is that we often do know enough to know which views count as reasonable without knowing which view counts as right, and this point is sufficient to allow people to construct deliberative processes that should correct for the most serious problems potentially created by group polarization. What is necessary is not to allow every view to be heard, but to ensure that no single view is so widely heard, and reinforced, that people are unable to engage in critical evaluation of the reasonable competitors. The value of deliberation, as a social practice, depends very much on social context—on the nature of the process and the nature of the participants. Here, institutions are crucial.

One of the most important lessons is among the most general. It is crucial to create spaces for enclave deliberation without insulating enclave members from those with opposing views, and without insulating those outside of the enclave from the views of those within it. While group polarization, produced by deliberation among like-minded people, is a potential threat to sense and stability, it can also be enlisted in the interest of both. In the United States, both checks and balances and federalism are exemplary efforts in this vein, and the twenty-first century should see many creative efforts to create institutional innovations with the same fundamental goals.

Notes

1. See Roger Brown, *Social Psychology: The Second Edition* (New York: The Free Press, 1985), 203–26.

2. Ibid., 204.

3. Ibid., 224.

4. David G. Myers and George D. Bishop, "Discussion Effects on Racial Attitudes," *Science* 169, no. 3947 (1970): 778–79.

5. See Albert Breton and Silvana Dalmazzone, "Information Control, Loss of Autonomy, and the Emergence of Political Extremism," in *Political Extremism and Rationality*, ed. Albert Bretton et al. (Cambridge: Cambridge University Press, 2002), 53–55.

6. See Reid Hastie, David Schkade, and Cass R. Sunstein, "What Happened On Deliberation Day?" *California Law Review* 95 (2007): 915–45.

7. These examples are taken from Cass R. Sunstein et al., *Are Judges Political? An Empirical Investigation* (Washington, DC: Brookings Institution, 2005).

8. See Thomas Miles and Cass R. Sunstein, "The Real World of Arbitrariness Review," *University of Chicago Law Review* 75 (forthcoming).

9. See Cass R. Sunstein et al., *Punitive Damages: How Juries Decide* (Chicago: University of Chicago Press, 2007).

10. See ibid.

11. For a relevant discussion of why polarization occurs, see Brown, *Social Psychology*, 200–245.

12. See Robert Baron et al., "Social Corroboration and Opinion Extremity," *Journal of Experimental Social Psychology* 32 (1996): 537.

13. See Mark Kelman et al., "Context-Dependence in Legal Decision Making," *Journal of Legal Studies* 25 (1996): 287–88.

14. Baron et al., "Social Corroboration," 537.

15. See Chip Heath and Richard Gonzales, "Interaction with Others Increases Decision Confidence But Not Decision Quality: Evidence Against Information Collection Views of Interactive Decision Making," *Organizational Behavior and Human Decision Processes* 61 (1997): 305–26.

16. Ibid. It has similarly been suggested that majorities are especially potent because people do not want to incur the wrath, or lose the favor, of large numbers of people, and that when minorities have influence, it is because they produce genuine attitudinal change. See Baron et al., "Social Corroboration," 82. The demonstrated fact that minorities influence privately held views on such contested issues as gay rights and abortion (ibid., 80) attests to the value of creating institutions that allow room for diverse voices.

17. See R. T Riley and T. F Pettigrew, "Dramatic Events and Attitude Change," *Journal of Personality and Social Psychology* 34 (1976): 1004.

18. See Arnold Jacobs, *Race, Media, and the Crisis of Civil Society* (Cambridge: Cambridge University Press, 2001), 144.

19. See Cass R. Sunstein, *Republic.com 2.0* (Princeton, NJ: Princeton University Press, 2007).

20. See Patricia Wallace, *The Psychology of the Internet* (Cambridge: Cambridge University Press, 2000), 73–84.

21. See Jürgen Habermas, "Between Facts and Norms: An Author's Reflections," *Denver University Law Review* 76 (1999): 937, 940–41.

22. See Caryn Christensen and Ann S. Abbott, "Team Medical Decision Making," in *Decision Making in Health Care*, ed. Gretchen B. Chapman and Frank A. Sonnenberg (Cambridge: Cambridge University Press, 2000), 267, 273.

23. Ibid., 274.

24. C. Kirchmeyer and A. Cohen, "Multicultural Groups: Their Performance and Reactions With Constructive Conflict," *Group and Organization Management* 17 (1992): 153.

25. Edmund Burke, "Speech to the Electors" (Nov. 3, 1774), in *Burke's Politics*, ed. R. Hoffman and P. Levack (London, 1949), 116.

26. See *The Federalist* no. 10.

27. See Cass R. Sunstein, "Interest Groups in American Public Law," *Stanford Law Review* 38 (1985): 29, 42.

28. See Jürgen Habermas, *The Structural Transformation of the Public Sphere* (Cambridge, MA: MIT Press, 1991), 231–50.

29. See Anne Phillips, *The Politics of Presence* (Oxford: Oxford University Press, 1995); Cass R. Sunstein, "Beyond the Republican Revival," *Yale Law Journal* 97 (1988):1539, 1585–89.

About the Author

Cass R. Sunstein is the Felix Frankfurter Professor of Law at Harvard Law School. He was formerly the Karl N. Llewellyn Distinguished Service Professor of Jurisprudence at the University of Chicago, where he maintains an affiliation as a visiting professor. Before joining the faculty of the University of Chicago Law School, he worked as an attorney-adviser in the Office of Legal Counsel at the U.S. Department of Justice. He is a former law clerk to Justice Thurgood Marshall. Mr. Sunstein has testified before congressional committees on many subjects and has been involved in constitution-making and law reform activities in a number of nations, including Ukraine, Poland, China, South Africa, and Russia. A member of the American Academy of Arts and Sciences, Mr. Sunstein has served as the Samuel Rubin Visiting Professor of Law at Columbia Law School, a visiting professor of law at Harvard Law School, vice chair of the American Bar Association (ABA) Committee on Separation of Powers and Governmental Organizations, chair of the Administrative Law Section of the Association of American Law Schools, a member of the ABA committee on the future of the Federal Trade Commission, and a member of the President's Advisory Committee on the Public Service Obligations of Digital Television Broadcasters.

Mr. Sunstein's books include *After the Rights Revolution* (Harvard University Press, 1990), *Free Markets and Social Justice* (Oxford University Press, 1997), *Laws of Fear: Beyond the Precautionary Principle* (Harvard University Press, 2005), *Republic.com 2.0* (Princeton University Press, 2007), and *Worst-Case Scenarios* (Harvard University Press, 2007). He is the coeditor of *Administrative Law and Regulatory Policy*

(Aspen Publishers, 1998). Mr. Sunstein's articles have appeared in the *Harvard Law Review*, the *Journal of Law & Economics*, the *New Republic*, and the *Wall Street Journal*, among others.

REG-MARKETS CENTER
AEI Center for Regulatory and Market Studies

The Reg-Markets Center focuses on understanding and improving regulation, market performance, and government policy. The Center provides analyses of key issues aimed at improving decisions in the public, private, and not-for-profit sectors. It builds on the success of the AEI-Brookings Joint Center for Regulatory Studies. The views expressed in this publication are those of the author.

ROBERT HAHN
Executive Director

Publications can be found at: www.reg-markets.org